THE PROPHET RETURNS

THE HIP HOP GENERATION REMIX OF A CLASSIC

BRYONN BAIN

THE PROPHET RETURNS

THE HIP HOP GENERATION REMIX OF A CLASSIC

BRYONN BAIN

EDITED BY SUHEIR HAMMAD

Blackout Brooklyn Press
Brooklyn, New York

Calligraphy by Maytha Alhassen

Designed by ARTHAMETRIC

Library of Congress Control Number: 2011909461
ISBN: 978-0-615-46982-9

"One of the leading minds of his generation, Bain speaks his truth with a power we desperately need to hear."

"...inspired by the writings of poets ranging from Rumi to Rakim Allah, The Prophet Returns is a spoken word epic in which the mystic teachings of the masters dance with the artistry of this new urban voice in a tale that pulsates tangibly in the now."

"I read an awful lot of work that cuts the edge the way The Prophet Returns does -- and I can honestly say that there's nothing out there like it. It's stunning. With the publication of this work, Bryonn will carve his own unique niche, at the juncture of song, speech and the gospel truth. I can't wait for the rest of the world to see it."

"...a spellbinding spoken word poet and thoughtful chronicler of the challenges facing black men. I cannot think of any student I have taught at either the University of Pennsylvania or Harvard Law School in the past 20 years who has Bryonn's range of talent and who uses those talents so selflessly."

A little while,
a moment of rest upon the wind,
and another woman shall bear me.

1923

CONTENTS

PROLOGUE

A prisoner rumored to have visions sat watching the shadows cast on his cell floor. As he ate the last meal of his lengthy sentence, his shadow spoke saying, *What strength your body has gained since you were taken captive so long ago. It seems you are better off indeed after having lost your liberty.* But the prisoner said nothing. For he thought it foolish to speak with his own shadow.

As midnight emerged under a full moon, the prisoner turned the final page of the last book he would read while confined. And his shadow spoke again saying, *How sharp your mind has grown since the wings of your freedom were severed long ago. It seems you are better off in thought after having been stripped of your freedom.* But the prisoner held his silence. For his soul was unmoved by what his shadow had to say.

When at last twilight turned to dawn, the prisoner grew overjoyed. And he kneeled in meditation on the words of the great Almustafa. Singing his most beloved verse of the Prophet aloud, he knew this would be his last recital in captivity. *Life is conceived in the mist, and not in the crystal.* Then his shadow spoke a third time saying, *So learned in the ways of the soul have you become since you were confined in this cage. It seems you are better off in spirit for having been held captive here so long.*

Vexed by this onslaught of insults, the prisoner stood over his shadow and spoke saying, *When the first-born sons of every village were threatened by the prophecy of darkness, I was jailed for burning the very bush that brought light to the prophets of old. How is a man engaged in the mystic rites of his ancestors better off confined by concrete and steel?*

And where was your wisdom years ago when I was given no choice but to protect my own life at the price of another? The boldest of those sworn to serve and protect found himself at the edge of his own weapon that very evening. Is he better off as well?

But his shadow only shrugged. So the prisoner spoke once more, saying in a loud voice, *I was of divine blood when sent to this dungeon years ago. Those guilty of survival are not better off for time spent caged like savage beasts. And the world beyond these walls is worse off without the blessing of our lessons learned.*

Jalil had hardly uttered his last word when his shadow morphed into an elephant with three eyes over its rising trunk. A necklace of braided scarlet serpents slithering around her neck. The beast was of that mystic race of fire known to mortals as the Jinn. And she mocked the prisoner in a thunderous voice saying, *You were a murderer just yesterday. Tomorrow you will be a free man. The food you were fed, the books you have read, and the guidance your soul has received inspired the dreams delivering you to freedom. Time seems to have weighed Justice' scales in your favor.*

The village you left so long ago is in need of the lessons learned from your suffering within these walls. You may remain here the rest of your days and be repaid the vast debt owed you, or end your captivity here tomorrow. And it will not have been in vain. But should you choose to leave, sirens will sound my return to remove you from the outer world by the next setting of the sun. For the world beyond these walls is a prison beyond prison. One without parole or pardon. And to the realm of shadows shall you escape, once your light has shone once more on the path of those who lit your own.

Upon returning to his village, those who learned of the visions that set him free hailed the prisoner a prophet. Those who overheard his conversations with shadows, condemned him a madman the balance of his days.

THE FAREWELL

Jalil, the chosen and beloved, waited thirty three years to return to the village of his birth. At the end of his thirty third year in prison, on the morning of the seventh day of Ramadan, the prayers of his elders and ancestors arrived to carry him home. The cage that held him captive was flung open. And his joy flew freely over land and sea unseen by him for nearly half his lifetime.

Before he bid his cellmates farewell, the heart beating within him whispered to his mind saying, *How am I to go without sorrow? Long nights have I spent tormented within these walls finding comfort only in the certainty of my Solitude. And who can depart Solitude without regret? It is not a fresh set of clothes I put on in leaving this place, but an old unfamiliar skin I once wore. It is a skin in which I am not seen as I am. A skin that masks the shape and size of my spirit from those whose gaze I meet.*

Yet I can linger within this brick and mortar dungeon no longer. The world calls for me now and I must obey. I would take with me all I have here, but how can I? Without her cocoon must the butterfly sail the summer wind into the horizon and watch the sun bathe in a sea of sky.

As he looked upon the other inmates for the last time, his soul cried out to them saying, *Brethren, together we have longed to see the face of Freedom. How often has this day come to us in our dreams? And now it has come to me in a slumber I pray will never end. I am ready as ever now to go. With the hungry patience of a shotgun locked and loaded, I await the firing of that reluctant assassin called Justice. For at last she has chosen to launch me toward the target of a tomorrow beyond these bars. Only another breath am I to breathe of this stale air. Only another embrace am I to share with this iron maiden. Then I will walk among the women and children of my village once more.*

The subway train rumbled into Atlantic Terminal and Jalil stepped into a village like none known to him before. It was as if downtown Brooklyn was withering away from a sickness unseen. The streets of his beloved Medina greeted him now for the first time since its symptoms spread. Sights and sounds hardly heard by him in childhood had become the order of the day. Age dwelled upon the face of every child. Youth worn beyond its years marched in and out of storefront shops. Under the spell of the idols sought and carried around him, men and women blessed with abundance sang out to the heavens boastful of avarice and ignorance. The village appeared at war with Wisdom. Virtue crouched in submission at the feet of Vice. And the righteous hid from the wicked. Only elders with years long enough to remember the old ways remained unmoved by the savage manner of the day.

Walking past the majestic clock tower, the stroke of twelve reminded him of the grooming ritual once held in the village at this hour. But he was unaware this blessed day would gather his loved ones at the workplace of the most favored barber in Brooklyn. For though few spoke of it as such, this gathering of sages and scribes had long been a stem for the more fragrant flower of their togetherness. As he walked towards Fulton Street, faces in whose midst he was raised as a child hastened to bring themselves together for his homecoming. Old and young alike came to welcome the village griot home at last.

Resting on the marble steps of the Brooklyn Academy of Music, an elderly woman wore her years as a dove's finest feathers. Hamida Mohammed was the eldest Priestess in the village. And Jalil looked upon her overjoyed. Though his irreverence as a child seldom allowed him to sit in the solace of her home, it was the Priestess who first revealed his gift to him. For he was but a boy then, and had not yet come to believe.

Then the Priestess hailed him saying, *Prophet of Medina, long have we awaited the day that would return you to us. At last our prayers have brought you back to the village of your birth. The village is in need of your voice now more than ever. Deep is our longing to drink from the streams you have been submerged in since our separation. Vast is our yearning for the insight you possess. Since you last stood at our side, countless youth have been taken captive. And ours is among hundreds of villages pillaged since you were imprisoned.*

A small crowd of construction workers, school children, suited women and men sat on the Academy steps. And every ear stopped to listen as the Priestess spoke with an enchanting voice.

The spirit of our village is held captive. In a prison that has separated us from our selves as you and others have been as well. But what freed you and returned your gift possesses the power to free us all.

This alone do we ask: that you speak your truth to us this day. Feed us the ripe fruit from the abundant fields and vineyards of your understanding. For we will pass it unto nearby villages, and they to neighboring provinces, and they to lands beyond our borders. And your Word will spread like a rippling wave in an endless ocean echoing the world over. Your song will be sung to our children and to their children. And you will not perish.

Jalil bent his head and barely held back the well rising within. And he answered saying, *People of Medina, what can I say that is not already beating in the chambers of your hearts and blowing through the winds of your imagination?*

ON THE DIVINE

Then the Priestess spoke saying, *It is written: God is One. But the Spirit has many windows, through which it can be seen by every searching eye. And many doorways, for those willing to enter. Though we struggle to divide ourselves and the Divine into fragments, to the Oneness we return.*

What say you of the Divine?

Raising his head, the Poet looked upon the villagers gathered around him. And as a stillness fell upon them, he spoke with a great voice saying:

> When I never seen
> The scriptures encrypted
> In the leaves of trees
>
> When I never heard
> Hymns hummed in harmony
> By a colony of bees
>
> When I never learned
> Elders are angels
> Sent to watch over me
>
> I used to worship in the Temple
> Sacrifice in the Sanctuary
>
> But in my youth
> I got the gospel Truth
> From a blade of grass

Witnessed the wisdom
Of the water
Running in my bath

Wind was my religion
Telling the future of my past
I used to worship in the Temple

I used to recite psalms in the Synagogue

Until a woman
Who had a way with words
Made me want to do away with words

Performed poetry on me
Without saying
A single word

Strumming sonnets
On the strings that sing
The song of my manhood

Strumming sonnets
On the strings that sing
The song of my soul

As good
As worship in the Temple
I used to worship in the Temple

I used to sing suras in the Mosque

Where Karma couldn't
Catch a cab on the corner of the Cross
Unless she double-crossed Krishna

For thirty pieces of Shiva

Meditated with mantras under mangos
Contemplated Siddhartha under a kangol
Cause a kangol looks like a halo on a negro

Whenever we go
Out to eat
Angel hair pasta

Or sit beside a Rasta
Blasting reggae remixes of Rumi
Out his radio and translating Revelations

Back into Ebonics
From Ibo
Before chanting

Nam
Myoho
Renge kyo

Old school jive for
Everything is everything
Cause everything says so

Holy water pours no holier
Than the water in your well
Right now

Church bells sound
No more sacred than
Cowry shells on the ground

Rosary beads
Come no closer to heaven
Than a bag of trees somehow

Yesterday and Tomorrow
Come and go
No holier than now

Buddha comes back
In the newborn body
Of a blue-black baby

Saint Mary becomes blind
Crippled and crazy
Lives out of a box

As an old bag lady

Shango shoots up tornadoes
To shoot the breeze
With Jesus Christ

Persephone and Ogun
Ménage with the Moon
Soon as you go to bed at night

But I see

SKIES OF BLUE

Have you gotten
The gospel Truth
From a blade of grass?

CLOUDS OF WHITE

Witnessed the wisdom
Of the water
Running in your bath?

BRIGHT BLESSED DAYS

Is wind your religion
Telling the future
Of your past?

DARK SACRED NIGHTS

I used to worship in the Temple

AND I THINK TO MYSELF

I used to sacrifice in the Sanctuary

WHAT A WONDERFUL WORLD

I used to recite psalms in the Synagogue

AND I THINK TO MYSELF

I used to sing suras in the Mosque

WHAT A WONDERFUL WORLD

I used to worship in the Temple

Until I realized

EVERYTHING AROUND ME IS GOD

ON RELIGION

A Temple, a Mosque and a Synagogue

Sat conversing in peace as the Sun skated across the horizon.

Overhearing their gentle conversation,

the Creator interrupted saying:

What a blessing
You understand and speak
My language so very fluently.

What a pity
Those gathered in your midst
Forgot how so very long ago.

ON DECEPTION

On a hand-carved mahogany stool beside the Ital Shack, a lanky old Rastaman sat burning frankincense and kush. A bushy mane framed his sun-kissed Kingston face. Unbraided locks of ebony dangled down his back like a runaway comet's tail. Though the offering that swirled skyward from the table before him was his craft, he was as versed in the science of the stars. Spying those that had gathered around the Poet at the corner of Fulton and St. Felix, the Rasta's rumbling baritone roared out to the Poet.

And he spoke saying, *Jah sends warnings inscribed on parchment for the wicked to hold in his hand, but a stubborn eye deceives him into reading signs and symbols as mere sorcery. The false prophet comes to souls thirsty for salvation like clouds over the Sahara without a single drop of rain. And the deceitful conceal foul intentions with a flowery lie dressed in the drag of Truth.*

What say you of Deception?

And the Poet answered saying:

Ignorance
Rocks dread locks
Sometimes

Self-hate

Slaps head wraps
Around relaxed naps
So you can't see

What's on her mind
What lies on her mind
When lye is on her mind

Intellect
Gets out a bat
To protect her neck

Get God's back

Leaving religions
Bludgeoned to death
By the dozen

For pretending
To be
Spirituality

When most can't even be
As close as distant
Cousins

Cause in
Spite of the reality
That spirituality is relative

Religion and Spirituality
Are not necessarily relatives
Though they often seem related

Things
Are often not
What they seem

Things
Fall apart
When pulled apart

By what?

Seams

Things fall apart
When pulled apart
By what seems

What seems
Is something
Our senses dream

Takes more than common sense
To make sense of
A common dream

Some dreams only youth hear

As Age turns Time's pages
Elders lose their ears
To their heirs

Forget their fear
Of failing to fulfill
Fantasies that will forever

Disappear

We can't let
Their fantasies disappear
We can't let our imagination disappear

If we do then

What the hell
On earth
We doing here?

Been to earth
Never been to hell
But if I had been there

I imagine
It would be a nation
With no imagination

Imagine
It would be a nation
Where every nationality is Reality

Imagine
In this image of a nation
In my imagination

If everybody fell to hell
We'd all be forced
To keep it real

Since Reality somehow
Hypnotizes everybody
Kidnaps Creativity

Got niggas thinking
We can only be
What we see

But we don't
Have to be only
What eyes can see

You can keep it real
If you want to keep it real
I ain't trying to keep it real

Reality is killing me
I'd rather swim
In a fantasea

Or stand in a metaforest
Planting my own poetree
Stirring a piping hot pot of possibilitea

With honey please
Wherever my honey be
Not like the insect

But like existence BE
Letting me be
Who I be

So I can be
We can be
All we can be

We can all be free

If we can just set free
What it means to be
Or not to be

Existence
Should not be shackled
By any one word or definition

Existence should not be shackled
By anyone's words or definitions
Definitions are for definers

Not for the defined
Definitions are for definers
Not for the Divine

Definitions definitely ain't divine

You can't define
Anything divine
With any definition you can find

What you can find is a long line of definers
Who have lost they damn minds
Trying to define my behind

Since before the birth of Time
When we sold Earth solid gold
Told her son to shine

Made the moon swoon
With a swig of her own moonshine
She still can't walk a straight line anymore

Stumbles in circular motions
Shaking the ocean's floor
Back and forth

Forth and back
Gets so dizzy
She sees black

Gets so dizzy
Everything
Goes black

Once you go blackward
You never go back
Word

You only go blackward
The blackest word
I ever heard was

WE

So I turn it
Upside down
Use it interchangeably with ME

Things are often not what they seem

ON TRUTH

الحقيقة

Next door to the Brooklyn Moon Cafe, a fire hydrant noticed the noon sun soaking up a puddle and began to cry. *Why waste your tears, old friend?* said the Puddle to the Hydrant. *The storm cloud promises my swift return from the sky.*

Yes, replied the Hydrant with watery eyes. *Such is your truth. It comes and goes with the sun ray and the storm cloud, reminding you of your seen and unseen self. But what of my truth? It hides beneath this cage of steel restless as you rise in the mist and travel telling your own to distant lands.*

The Puddle pondered his old friend's question. Then spoke saying, *Your truth is the same as that of your Maker. Ever present, but uttered only on occasion of great joy or sorrow. It is a sacred offering to tame the scorching flame or quench Summer's thirst.*

But I return time and again that you might see your reflection and be reminded of your wealth within.

ON LIFE

As Jalil passed the Habana Outpost market, there came an Elder only days from having breath abandon his body. Now the Elder spoke to the Poet saying, *In the final hour every deed will be revealed from first to last. Those who have loved this fleeting world too well will reap the barren fields sown by living heedless of the world to come.*

Yet the scribes have also written that while the dead tremble before the tempest, the living walk in its midst. For the passing of life is not the end of the soul's journey, but only a new beginning. And the leaf that falls from the tree fertilizes its own resurrection.

What say you of Life?

And the Poet spoke saying:

Live each day
As if there is no tomorrow
To borrow a second chance from

Breathe each breath

As if with your last lung
When you and yours are on the run
From an avalanche weighing over a ton

Speak each word

As if spoken with a stolen tongue
Stolen from a hundred hungry hunters
Surrounding you with a hundred loaded guns

Climb each ladder

As if your hand landed
On the last rung as you rise
Into the sky to kiss the sun goodbye

Savor each kiss

As if your lips
Kissed God's left eye
Just as she goes blind and has to find someone

Who has seen things her way
To help redesign the universe
Back before time

And you just
Happen to be there
After meeting her in prayer

Pray each prayer

As if it is the last prayer
Anyone anywhere
Will ever say or hear

Pray for enough to share
With those around you
Not for enough to spare

As if next year said you will be here

Somebody say you'll be here another day
How do you know you'll be here another hour
Nobody knows if you will be here another minute

Experience each minute

As if an eternity lives in it
A thousand lifetimes will be behind you
After each minute has finished

Finish each meal

As if each morsel of each mouthful
Carries the last sensation
Your senses will ever feel

From forehead to heel

Feel each caress of your skin
As if you never knew flesh
In this world full of sin

This world full of shame
A world full of pain
A world where

Pleasure is the last remaining measure
Of a long lost science
Called Love

Buried at the bottom of a sea of secrets
In a silver treasure chest
But we are the pirates

We are the pilots
We are the deep sea divers
Who know these waters best

Give your best when you give at all
As if to give any less of yourself
Brings the fall of humankind

That kind of unkind kindness
Is better off unborn in a mind
Than born in a word or deed

The world doesn't need

What the world needs
Is for you to believe
Every deed matters

Your every word matters more than you imagine

Imagine
This moment is the one
You lived your life to get to

It is

Imagine this moment
Is the final door
Your feet will step through

Might be

If you left your life this very moment
Why would you have shed your last tear
Where would you have fought your last fight

Whose would be
The last face you faced
In the middle of your very last night

Care for those
Who care for you
As if the present is a gift

The future gives
No second chance
To steal a second glance from

Make love to your beloved
As if there is no next time
To rescue romance from

Love to live as if not to
Only gives Death
A chance to cheat you

Before he greets you into the afterlife
Live each moment of your life
As if it is your very last

And go to the grave knowing
You took nothing
For granted

ON DEATH

Before the Poet had made his way past Moshood's Boutique, there came a wounded Soldier on his way home from war. One who was forced to bury his younger brother on the battlefield in a ditch they dug together. Mud and tears masalaed together under nine fingernails lingering without the thumb he lost to a land mine.

And the Soldier spoke saying, *Who can live and not be devoured by death? Brave men claim the soul passes away with the body forever. And doubt man is made of that energy which can neither be created nor destroyed. But the prophets of old said the song of the sea ends not at the shore, but in the hearts of those who hear it sung. Death is only a soul shedding its skin like a winter coat in summer weather. And the spirit longs to kiss the sun as does the earth a falling feather.*

What say you of Death?

And the Poet answered the Soldier saying:

Like the sailor
Sees the sirens
Through their song

The soul can be seen
Sentenced to life
Inside your body

Reincarnated
To be incarcerated
In this cage called flesh

Released on probation
Only through meditation
A morse code made by men

On the other side of the tracks
In the arm of a heroine
Committing heresy against herself

By myself
In the womb
Like I was in the tomb

I died free
Wasn't born to live life a slave
Now I am back from the grave

In a rage
To get mine
We be divine

Not just some ebonic line
We transcend space and time
Who else sends Space back in time

Sends Time back home to recline
Ain't a damn thing they can do
To hold back me and mine

Kill me soft
Hang me on a cross
Or cut my head off black

- One time -

No loss
Everything
Comes back black

- Two times -

Better believe that

I bleed the same blood
Put Goliath on his back
With a stone from that sack

Way back black
- That's three -
Three blacks

The trinity must be back
Not just God the Father
Beside God the Son

Like Holy Mother's ghost
Somewhere
Shooting smack

Burning glass viles of that
White powder cotton candy
Cops can't seem to crack

Talking about
They don't know
Where it comes from

Talking about
They don't know
Where it's at

Just like Uncle Tom
As a matter of fact
Has no clue

Where he come from
Yes Massa?
No idea where he at

Yes Boss?
Don't know where he going…
Massa?

Going…
Boss?
Gone are the days

When the ignorant slave
Celebrates the chains
Trapping him in his Socratic cave

As he breaks free
Out of the cave his eyes see
We have always been and will always be

MC's
Go back before M.C.C.
Numerically that's twelve century A.D.

Age of Darkness
But in the dark ages
Wasn't we who was sparkless

We sparked it like an L
Lit on flames in hell
Kept it bright

Kept it right
Kept the Romans real
They was on that i i i shit

While we was like
1   2   3
Letting them know the deal?

We brought the light and sun
Son, we brung the sages
Now we out here dying

For minimal wages

Outrageous as it sounds
Those who bound us
Adore us

As if Osirus throne
Was overthrown
By young Horus

But they warned us
Before just check
Psychology texts

Son kills father
Oedipus Rex
Complex?

Yes

I was reincarnated to be incarcerated
In this cage called flesh
All that Death can do

Is set me free

ON WORK

From under the glass ornamented doorway of Cake Man Raven's Confectionary, there came a Keeper of Gardens. And he spoke to the Poet saying, *It is written: those who till the land taste the sweetest bread. Though the slothful and sluggard crave, they slumber during harvest and sleep through the hunt. Then wonder why the diligent are supplied precious wealth.*

But have the prophets of old not instructed that one who works without joy is better off leaving work alone to beg charity of those who work with love? To bemoan the mashing of apples distills bitter poison in the cider.

What say you of Work?

And the Poet answered saying:

Work is spirit igniting flesh
A flame set ablaze
By every breath

Plant Passion in open fields of Faith
By midseason your barren garden
Will be overgrown

Water your Wants and Needs
With buckets filled
At Wisdom's well

Watch Absence
Blossom into orchards
Of Abundance and Satisfaction

Sow the seeds of Sorrow
In the fertile earth of friendship
Reap a harvest of Happiness and Laughter

Heartier than heaven ever heard

Cast your empty net
In rivers of Regret
With words hooked on Hatred

Witness your heart go hungry
Though both your hands
Will be filled

Aim your arrow
Tipped with Arrogance
At the tender limbs of a lover

Her body will bleed
Streams of insecurity
The same color as your own blood

Bury grudges
In an open casket
Crafted by Cowardice

You will fertilize the earth
Carrying and giving birth
To the worst of your fears

The wealthy banker
Shackled to a soulless desk
Whispers to himself in secret

Labor is a wretched curse

The humble hunter
Possessed by no possession
Surveys the jungle singing overjoyed

Labor is the richest blessing

ON FEAR

Then came a young Girl who gifted him a sunflower. As the Poet stopped to rest beside the bodega on Clinton Avenue, the child confessed she had been frightened by the silhouette of the flower at first sight. Skirted in blue-gray plaid, the Girl told how she knelt in the center of Prospect Park to gather his gift. But when another sunflower's shadow stretched towards her, it appeared in the shape of a cobra's crown. And she fled at once in fear.

And the young Girl spoke saying, *Those who walk without fear stray from the righteous path. But is it not also written that we must live with courage for the Creator is with us always? And what greater obstacle to love is there than fear? Yet those who live and love fearlessly are like the moth fluttering alongside the flame unafraid of death.*

What say you of Fear?

With a sadness in his heart, the Poet answered saying:

Fear is on a mission

Inflicting infectious diseases
Like Dogma and Doubt
Throughout

What Might Be

Until What Might Be
Lays the empty egg
Cynicism scrambles to feed Failure

From the time
He finds Failure
Lying in the fetal position

Fear is on a mission
But Bravery lives beyond Fear
And Courage is on a mission of her own

To wave metaphor
Like a matador's red cape
Until her tongue teaches anyone

Afraid of the Impossibull
Escape routes through speech
Spoken in the language of the subconscious

Consciously seeping in constantly
Like a sandcastle city
Sculpted in the quicksands of Time

Where citizens
Run trains of thought
Off of one track minds

Conviction is on a mission
To capture that kleptomaniac
Cousin of Fear

Some call Procrastination
Who has stolen moments from Night and Day
Hijacked excuses to make his getaway

Dreams are on a mission
To walk the plank with Profanity
Without worrying whether they will drown

Turning around
Semantic straightjackets
Into linguistic lifejackets

Proving the profane can be profound
Like bad can be damn good
Left can be right or wrong

Saints go marching into
The underground to drop bombs
Where sinners flee God forsaken jobs

Come catch the spirit just as hard
As a séance on Sabbath
Inside of the synagogue

Where a DJ drops it on the one
For the ONE is the only God
For 12 inch disciples of ancient old school beats

Raising hell nonstop in shell-top sandaled feet
Spinning on and on til the break of Don Quixote
Who windmills whenever the beat comes on

Whenever two turntables
Come together to impregnate Silence
With sound decibels daring to resurrect

The dead of night

Word is born
And born again like Christ
The beat goes on and on and on

Like everlasting life

I am on a mission
To sing the song that is unheard of
Look at city pigeons and see black doves

Behold the tree

Knows not the secret
Thinks his branches
Meant for lynching limbs

Behold the cocoon

Holds the secret
But knows not
What she holds

Behold the caterpillar

Knows not the secret
Thinks the skyline
Sculpted for the mountain

Behold the tree
That holds the cocoon

Behold the cocoon
That holds the caterpillar

Behold the caterpillar
That holds the secret

Behold the secret
You have nothing to fear

ON FAITH

الإيمان

Out of the alleyway behind Joloff Restaurant, there came a homeless Boy who fled his father's house the year before. The child's once brown feet were bare and blackened by the earth.

Nudging his way through the crowd gathered around the Poet, the Boy called out to him saying, *Is it not written that those who do good works in the fullness of faith will not be forgotten? I have walked amidst the faithless and remained faithful. Where is the morsel I am due for remaining steadfast? Why have I no cup overflowing with milk and honey? What offering have you to keep the groans of this empty belly of mine from drowning out the melody of my Faith?*

The Poet crouched beside the Boy, then reached into his knapsack and removed a cloth pouch. As he unwrapped its contents, the Poet spoke saying:

All I got is some fish
And a few loaves of bread
And a whole lot of folks to feed

But if seven seas
Were made in under
Seven days

If the first man
Was forgiven
When he misbehaved

If a twig was taken
From a tree by a dove
To a boat built before the flood

If a rainbow
Was erected
To send out the sign

That the world
Would get wet
With the fire next time

If someone was told
To sacrifice his own son
Then told to hold up

Just before he was done

Then the fish
And the bread
I just said

Is all I got

That's all I need
For me to get fed
And for me to feed

A whole lot of folks in need

They set me on fire
But when they looked back
I was standing with my brothers

Shadrack and Meshack

Threw down with an angel
All through the night
Then got him to bless me

When I won the fight

Then had to fight
My ten older brothers
For sweating my triple fat goose

Coat of many colors

Had this dream they hated
About them bowing to me
So they sold me out

To a band of bandits
Who later on landed
Near where the water

One day was commanded
To stop and drop
Before blowing its top

Up into the ship
I was in
When I got

This fish I found
While fishing around
Underwater

Where the daughter
Of a pharaoh once found
The child chosen to force the pharaoh

To free his folks from a foreign land

Or prepare for plagues across the land
Prepare every woman
Prepare every man

Child
All I had
Was that rod in my hand

All I got is this rod
And a God
They don't know

Now how the hell am I
Supposed to get pharaoh
To let us all go?

All I got is some fish
And a few loaves of bread
And a whole lot of folks to feed

But I believe

I can part the sea
Now and then
Then put it back together again

I believe

I can kill any giant dead
If I believe in my heart
Bust him upside his head

With a stone thrown from the sling we'd bring
Back before we lost our crowns
When we knew we was kings

Way back when we heard prophecy say
Something will save you
If you jump in the sea

We healed the sick and made the blind see
Miracles wasn't profit motivated
Like the medical industry

Back in the day
We believed in believing
Like priests believe in belief

We believed
Faith comes to us
In the night like a thief

Knocks out
Uncertainty's teeth
Puts to death our disbelief

The faith that forced
Pharaoh to end slavery
Tells me it's time my people was free

The faith that lived through leprosy
Is a faith that will outlive
HIV

The faith that gets mountains up out of bed
Is a faith I believe is able to spread
Two little fish and five loaves of bread

Feed all of the folk who got to get fed
Believe I can make wine
Out of tap water

Tap
Tango
Break dance

And walk on water

Who could this be?
Believe it or not
Just me

And believe it
Or not
I am We

And believe it or not
The fish and the bread
I just said is all we got

That's all we need

For us to get fed
And for us to feed
A whole lot of folks in need

ON GOOD & EVIL

الخير و
الشر

Through the towering oak doors of the Seminary on Marcy Avenue came a Holy Man. Tucked under the armpit of his ivory robe, a bundle of leather-bound books clung together.

And he spoke saying, *The apostles warned that neither the work of the wicked nor the righteous goes without reward. For it is written, the all-seeing eye peers into every heart keeping watch on virtue as much as vice. Yet there are those who call it good when they steal what another loves, and evil when what they love is stolen.*

What say you of Good and Evil?

And the Poet answered singing:

The world is so upside down
I dialed nine nine nine
And said

Operator put the Devil on the line
Too many people on this planet poor and dying
It's time somebody gave Satan piece of they mind

Devil had me on hold four hundred years
But my eye was on the prize
I kept the phone to my ear

When he clicked over
He said can I call you back my man?
I am on the other line with my Uncle Sam

Sam needed a hand with a business plan
He was mad one went bad
Back in Vietnam

So I said Yo

Just call me back in a couple of years
Wanted to tell him go to hell
But he was already there

Most people miss the Devil when he walks right by
They be looking for his tail or two horns in the sky
The Devil doesn't look demonic

He don't act deranged
Drives a red Iroc
Rocks Armani exchange

Met him on a sunny summer afternoon
Hanging out at my house about to barbecue
My brother was getting mad cause all I had was tofu

When Lu came through and grabbed a couple of brews

The devil got drunk about half past two
Seen him slip some bacon in the vegetarian stew
Stole some old lady's dentures so she couldn't chew

Kicked down a little kid wearing corrective shoes

But what I can't stand didn't go down there
Don't care that he be tripping after too many beers
What I hate is all the suffering that seems to surround me

Cause he got cash ruling everything around me

Got moms at three jobs just to make ends meet
My brother stabbed up in the street last week
My older cousin overdosing on cocaine

My homey took a bullet to the back of the brain

But I wasn't bout to stop when my phone call failed
Got out my PC to send the devil email
Copied his address off an old CD Rom

WickedMutherfuckerAngry@God.com

I
Wrote
Dear Devil

This letter is long overdue
It's time your wicked ways
Around the world was through

But before I got
Another word onto the keys
I heard beep beep beep beep

Now who the hell is this paging me?

Took my beeper off my hip
You won't believe what it said
Lucifer left you a message

Is all that it read

So I picked up a payphone
Started to retrieve the voicemail
Mephistopheles had left for me

He said sorry

I have not gotten back to you
But that ain't the only thing
I ain't been able to do

Been chillin like a villain
On vacation with my crew
On a beach in a black hole far from you

Looked up at the letter I nearly completed
Double clicked on an icon til it was deleted
The Devil hadn't been to earth in six centuries

The world is how it is
Cause that's how
People want it to be

Got my moms at three jobs just to make ends meet
The government don't give a damn if poor folks eat
My brother was stabbed up in the street last week
Another brother needed nikes on his feet

My older cousin overdosed on cocaine
Since Cointel Pro the ghetto ain't the same
My homey took a bullet to the back of the brain
NYPD wanted somebody to blame

We are living and dying
In this material world
Like spiritually anorexic boys and girls

ON THE FUTURE

الكونتيسة

The Skyscraper looked down on a Stray Cat and laughed saying, *Long ago your ancestor was a mighty ruler whose roar silenced a vast kingdom and shook every beast for miles. But today you run from pups and prey on puny rodents.*

The Stray Cat turned to the Skyscraper and smiled saying, *Your ancestor long ago was a towering mountain peak reaching into the heavens. Men and women sacrificed life and limb to scale to its summit. But today you are no more a challenge to climb than the flip of a single finger. Laugh if you like, but the modern world makes a mockery of us all. And between you and I, who deserves the bigger laugh?*

Across the street, a Blind Man sat listening on the cracked steps of the old Billie Holiday Theater. After hearing *the Poet and his followers in conversation, the Blind Man stood and called out to the Poet saying, Long after the last pyramid is leveled and the skyscrapers of the city stand no more, it is said the butterfly will float over the fields where the dewdrop glitters on the grass below.*

But is not the unfolding of our days and nights the secret knowledge of Time and Chance? For tomorrow's sunset is only for the horizon to see today.

What say you of the Future?

And the Poet answered saying:

Look into the future
The Bible comes out on CD Rom
With holographic Proverbs and interactive Psalms

Featuring prophets who preach profit maximization
As the disciples reload rifles
To get ready for Revelations

Moses marches back
From a broken promised land
Carrying photocopies of Pharaoh's chromosomes

In hands tattooed with plans
To clone Ramses' bones
Using photogenetics

Developed by
Demons disguised
As priests and rabbis

Who spray paint
Swastikas on pyramids
Since the planet's become anti-Kemetic

Look into the future

The Garden of Eden has been colonized
By serpents who feed us Apple pie lies
In the wild, wild West Bank

Where the Messiah is a madman
On the corner of Here and Now
Preaching to the people

Passing by about how...

Every instant
Is an infant
Turning into an eternity

A moment
Becomes a millennium
Seconds become a century

An insignificant idea in its infancy
Becomes the infinite currency
You memory bank on

To buy blind eyes some vision
Until they see Pessimism
Locks up Passion

In a poorly fashioned
Maximum security
Prison

Instead of flipping
The outcome of income
To come out right across the nation

Or pimping CEO's like hoes
To get underpaid workers
Overcompensation

Public school education
Subsidizes 21st century
Concentration camp incarceration

Meanwhile
The village idiot has become
The ruler of the world's most powerful nation

But look into the future

Where
Redemption Song
Is the national anthem

America
Has been going bankrupt
Paying back black Africa's ransom

Capitalism
Is so pissed
Humanity persists

The market bull sits
Parked in an alleyway
Slitting its bloody wrists

Multinational corporations grow vex

Waiting…
On online lines to cash
Corporate welfare checks

Poverty pushes paradigms like nickel bags
Got rich folks wrapped up
In filthy rags

Enslaved women
Dig up the graves of slave children
Who repay the ofay who ran the damn plantation

Hand me the forceps
Hand me the scalpel
Hand me the suture

The Past
Has gotten the Present
Pregnant with the Future

And She's about to deliver

Rivers to the desert
Freedom to the dungeons
Companions to the abandoned

Look
Into the future
We live in the future

The future is
A forgotten memory
In disguise

Tomorrow
Is born between
Today's thighs

The future is born
The moment we
Open our eyes

ON HOPE

On her way from the Egyptian Halal buffet to Abu's bakery, a Widow heard of the Poet's return and ran down Fulton until she reached him. The passing of her husband had announced itself every Winter for three years before ridding the loyal woman of her bedridden mate.

Catching her breath, she spoke saying, *It is written that suffering begets character, and character begets hope. The doubtful ask where one can witness hope at work. Some hope only for what can be seen. The sober mind is ever hopeful of the unseen. Like a reed bending in the wind, hope bows down and rises again. And those who hold on to hope survive the storm.*

But is it not also written that the most hopeful servant of God on earth was once afflicted with devastating misfortune? Was he not blameless when his property was stolen and his children slain? The rains of despair weather even the mightiest stone.

What say you of Hope?

And the Poet answered saying:

If the army ant
Marches for miles
With legs not so long

If the beetle loses
In battle with a boulder
Then has strength to press on

If the blue jay
With a broken wing
Sings his sweetest song

If the oak tree
Stands tall through fall
Though all her leaves be gone

If Day gets beat by Night
But stands on his feet
To fight by dawn

Then maybe I
And maybe you
Can find hope to carry on

ON PURPOSE

الكبب

Under the traffic light on Kingston Avenue, a frustrated
Spider spoke to a friendly Parking Meter.

*I guard mankind against the overcrowding of pests by filling
my belly each day. Man owes me for this service a debt I am
rarely rewarded. For he is blind to the gifts of Nature. But
you, dear Meter, are his own creation. And yet he curses you
daily. Have you not served your purpose well?*

Said the Parking Meter to the Spider, *You are most
observant. No doubt, dear Spider, you serve your purpose so
well. It seems mankind is not blind to the gifts of Nature
alone, but even to those he gives unto himself.
For my purpose and paradox are the same as yours.*

*I, too, stand guard and protect him from overcrowding.
But rather than applause from those my work benefits,
I am accused of greed whenever I fill my belly.*

ON POETS

الشعر

A shiny red milk crate sat outside Li's Chinese Restaurant. And there, collecting fortunes discarded between Albany and Throop, stood a Storyteller. Henna brought by a patron from Hyderabad traced stories yet untold from his wrists to the tips of his fingers. For he sketched tales on his hands in the ink of the ancients before sharing them with any person or page.

And the Storyteller spoke to the crowd walking alongside Jalil saying, *Poets have for centuries etched masterpieces on the canvas of the mind and scribed psalms on the papyrus of the heart. The griots of old spoke of one who stood between opposing armies and recited verse after verse with a resounding voice until the soldiers surrounding him threw down their weapons in tears. Lifelong enemies embraced with eyes weeping for joy.*

Yet it is also written that erring men follow the Poet as he roams the land aimlessly preaching what he never practices. Is your poetry a breath of light into the darkness? Or merely a product to be bought and sold? Was it not foretold that poets would one day fight for freedom of speech and press without anything fit to say or write? Have the Poets of today become ensnared by the vain utterances of their own careless mouths? Trapped in the idle scratching of unguided ink?

What say you of Poets?

And the Poet answered saying:

Justice
Sits handcuffed
In the back of an armored car

Freedom
Stands gagged
With a flag of fifty stars

Truth
Shouts locked down
With her lyrics behind bars

As the world
Wonders where
The hell on earth you are

Calling all MCs
Come in MCs
Come in

Calling verse writers
All improvisers of poetry
Master painters of lyrical calligraphy

Every second another deadly weapon comes to be
But the Word holds the most powerful weaponry
If a poem from the dome can part the Red Sea

A poem to the dome
Can make the blind see
Set the mind free

Call for balance with your talents
Or they will be seized
Write psalms to right wrongs

Seen on the daily
Since back before
The savagery of chattel slavery

Sing the song
Of the caged bird
Why James Byrds sing

Lynch ropes
Leave bloody rings
Round throats and collars

Makes me want to holler
Fools in power hardly bother
To think anything of suffering

Unless a string is dangling the dollar

Calling all MCs
Come in MCs
Come in

Do you copy
Can you copy
You know you copy

Copy
The Miner's Canary
Born to be an MC

Never sings
For no dime
She sings to be free

If you rhyme
For that dime
Why not to be free

In this land
Where women die
In the hands of Genocide

Nowhere to run or hide
From back alleys
To mountainsides

The innocent man still hangs from a tree
Give me a reason for treason to be
Unreasonable to me

Calling all MCs
Come in MCs
Come in

ON PRISON

Stumbling out of the youngest Brooklyn court building, there came a Mother with tears in her eyes. Her son had been sentenced for pinching the produce of a wealthy shopkeeper.

And the Mother cried out saying, *The rich justify the thievery that builds their wealth, and jail the penniless child who steals to feed himself. Yet it is also said the righteous are thrown into jail that they might be tested. And those who suffer for the sake of righteousness will be greatly blessed.*

But what of the spirit beckoning us toward justice? It demands the liberty of those unjustly taken captive and the freedom of the wrongfully bound.

What say you of Prison?

And the Poet answered saying:

>Prison bricks and mortar
>Swallow sons and daughters
>Make your run for the border
>
>The warden will send for you
>
>Over land and sea
>Like government property
>No body in this skin I'm in

Ever seen Liberty
Heard they got her body
Swinging from a bloody tree

In the land of the free
Where they hang Bravery
With the same chains

Men came to claim us with in slavery

Ancestors prayed
Day after day
Down on bended knee

Lord tell us we
Did not come here to stay
We just guests in this galaxy

Here for the day

Soldiers from a solar system light years away
Formed this flesh uniform from clay
When it gets torn we be on our way

We are and so I am
We were even back when
The Earth never knew men

When Now never knew Then

When Adam was just an atom
Matter just began to matter
DNA was just a ladder

We built to climb the heavens

We only became black
To practice coming back
Knew if we came like this

They'd crucify us like that
Incarcerate us like this
Execute us like that

Emulate us like this
Too late now
We coming back

Karma stays strapped
Carries a full pack
Unloads the whole clip

She holds to her hip
Backpack full of grenades
Homemade for slave ships

To save a slave whipped
Lashed for giving lip
Harassed for having hips

Hated for being hip
Shot for trying to run
Hung for trying to run

Hung for being hung
Beaten before your daughter
Gunned down in front your son

Until that final day
Your spirit says
I am done

I did not come here to stay
Just guests in this galaxy
Here for the day

Soldiers from a solar system light years away
Formed this flesh uniform from clay
When it gets torn we be on our way

Tell mama not to mourn
Every soul is reborn
We on our way

ON PARENTS

In the entrance of the barber shop on Marcus Garvey Boulevard, there stood a proud Father with a newborn wrapped in silk and resting in his arms.

Rasheed was the Poet's inseparable childhood friend, and the owner of this shop the crowd had walked so long to reach. The Poet embraced his best friend's daughter, Olori, and for the first time caressed the dimpled cheek of his godchild. A lone tear swam into the black thicket of his beard as he held her.

And Rasheed spoke saying, *Old friend, the ancients taught us ages ago to raise children as the jeweler engraves his most precious gem. For it is written: if you train a child in the way she should walk, Age will act as a guide along that path.*

Yet have the prophets not written the children we birth are not our own, but the sons and daughters of Life's longing for itself? For the mighty Marksman aims each child through adolescence towards adulthood and into the afterlife.

What say you of Parents?

And the Poet answered saying:

> Sea men sailed
> Over the waterfalls
> Of her vaginal walls

Our soul boats
Floated into her
Fallopian harbor

Where together
We became one
Forever

Born of my blood
Dressed in her flesh
Once nothing but mud

Now become nothing less than

The Sculptor's sculpture
Sculpting a sculpture of itself

The Painter's painting
Painting a painting of itself

Without a brush
Without canvas
Without the clay and perfect hands

God
Mother of man
Used to shape him

Never shed tears of joy
Before the day my boy was born
Understanding ran away with Dawn's first yawn

Wiping weeping eyes with a washcloth of laughter
I wonder am I the able servant of his smile
Or a shepherd guarding against disaster

Neither and Both

I am host in the house of Childhood
Here to let the guest alone
When in need of solitude to feel at home

Provide food and drink
Supply sufficient space
To sleep dream think

Keep open eyes
To witness the miracle
Of a spirit free at play

Open ears
To hear whatever
He may have to say

Open arms
Whenever his spirit
Strays into harm's way

Open mouth
Should the good Lord choose
To speak through me as we pray

Open mind
To that inevitable day
We will open doors

Watch our flesh and blood
Walk away with memories
I pray beg him one day to return

ON LOVE

Sunset swallowed by a famished sky, men, women and children gathered to make their way down the street to celebrate the Poet's return. At the end of his walk down the central artery of Medina, Jalil found himself surrounded by a cipher. The Priestess stood among the villagers assembled on the corner of Fulton and Malcolm X. And she called out to the Poet one last time saying, *Speak to us of Love.*

But before the Poet was able to answer, the Elderly man emerged once more from among the crowd. And he spoke saying, *Love is the sweetest fragrance known to man.* The Keeper of gardens approached and stood beside the Elder saying, *Love is the foulest odor ever known. Far more foul than the dung of elephants. But the fertile ground of the heart grows many fruits when planted with seeds of Patience, and watered with Wisdom and Faith.*

Love is an ocean that swallows the city of Reason whole, said the young Girl scared of shadows. *Love is a quenchless thirst,* replied the young Boy who fled his father's home chasing Pride. Then the Rastaman called out, *Love meditates in preparation for tomorrow. Love rejoices in song for today and laughs in remembrance of yesterday,* chimed the Storyteller.

But the young Father asked, *Is it not said Love reveals itself only at the hour of separation?* And the Preacher followed him proclaiming, *Love weeps for the wounded in the hour of injury.* And a Survivor responded, *Is it not written: Love knows its own bitterness, but no stranger shares its joy?* But the Poet kept his silence. His soul was moved beyond words by the villagers. For he knew their wisdom and his own were one and the same in Spirit and in Truth.

Then a young Lady in love spoke saying, *Love chooses nothing for itself. Love only longs to make choices possible for the beloved.* But the Widow shook her head saying, *Love gives no choice. Love knows no pity. Love is an incurable affliction and a malignant disease.* And the weeping Mother agreed saying, *The ancients warned the physician has no medicine for those sick with Love.*

But is Love not the marrow of Humanity? asked the School Teacher. *Like the blood in veins that feed our hearts, Love never forgets its source. How can we forget that Love is from where we came? Love and only Love asks us to be better than our best Self.* But the Soldier argued, *Love is the slow suffocation of common sense. A strangling with rope weaved together from threads drawn out the lover's own heart.*

But the Blind Man replied saying, *Love asks us to give of ourselves willingly and without regret. And we must give whatever Love asks with no regard for what will be given us in return. Should giving receive less glory than gain? One without the other cannot survive. Love is a raging river under an endless rainfall. Love both feeds and is fed always.*

Then at last the Poet spoke saying, *People of Medina, I have nothing to offer that is not already running within the rivers of your hearts and streaming between the shores of your souls. I possess no mysterious compass with which to guide you safely through the inevitable storms along the course of Love. No sorcery have I to siphon sap from the tree of Love's Suffering and Sorrow. I cast no spell to cure the anguish arising in the shadow of Her divine light. Of that magic I know nothing.*

But look to the words of the prophet Almustafa who told us that Love, if she finds you worthy, directs your course. For the prophets warn against the path of those who seek to embrace Love's Pleasure and escape her Pain. And the folly of those who long for lovers to laugh only half their laughter and weep only half their tears.

THE BEGINNING

البداية

Then the Priestess spoke to Jalil saying, *Bless this hour and the inspiration you have shared with us this day. How can we repay all you have given of yourself?* And he answered saying, *What should the flower price the pollen with which the bee makes her honey? How much should the clouds collect for the rains poured down to quench thirsting grass? Surely anyone worthy of her days and nights is worthy of whatever sound my words carry. For what I have to offer passes through me from a far greater source.*

You will return to us not a moment too soon, said the Priestess. *I pray you never keep your gift from others who yearn for understanding. Nor those who long to be reunited in the arms of the beloved. Tell us what must be done to end the captivity of our young? Ignore those who say in doubt the Divine never reveals anything to a mortal. Our liberation lingers like a fetus at the womb's edge of your word.*

Then the Poet spoke saying, *Let us not forget false prophets emerge with signs that lead astray even the elect. Who is more misleading than the man who says a prophecy was revealed to him when there has been no revelation? I am no more a messenger of the Divine than any of you now gathered here. Everything around me is God. So says spirit to flesh.*

What has been revealed to me was witnessed by those who came before in their own languages ages ago. I am a reflection of that which you helped me see during my days and nights in prison. The Universe sings her truth giving pause for no man. But the prisons we fashion around ourselves keep us from hearing her voice. I speak as a

151

reminder of her eternal teachings. Of that which was once known, but has been forgotten.

Prophet of Medina, asked the Priestess, *Why has the wisdom possessed by the ancients been forsaken? And what must we do to remind our village and others of what we have lost?*

And he answered saying, *Long ago our villages were pillaged of countless ancestors. Though the ransom was paid in excess, their kidnappers never returned them home. This is our story. And our story must be told.*

The wise Teacher instructs that we have forgotten from whence we came. Yet we have not taken heed. A blinding lust for the empty idols of the day keeps the village from seeing the danger of the path before us. Let us gather as one to build a pyre that each villager may cast into the flames whatever idol has come between our Love for one another.

No sooner had he spoken, than a bonfire was set ablaze in an empty steel drum at the end of the block. As it burned at the edge of Fulton Park, idols were brought from throughout the village and cast into the flames. Idols made of paper were thrown first for they were most abundant. Wooden and plastic idols were then consumed. Idols of clay and stone were next, followed by idols of steel, iron, brass, silver, gold and platinum. Last of all, those beset with rubies, emeralds, diamonds and pearls were thrown into the fire. A celebration erupted among the villagers as the idols danced their final number in the inferno.

But the festivity was hushed as sirens sounded in the distance. For the blaze caught the eye of men longing to return the Poet to the very prison where they had held him so many years. And though Jalil knew the sirenmakers would soon arrive as foretold, he refused to flee this place that had been made sacred by the fiery sacrifice of his loved ones.

People of Medina, he cried out with a mighty voice, the sirens summon me to leave you once again. Less hasty than they am I, but I must go. Each of us must some day be removed and scattered. I go now, but my journey is not in vain. Know that from amidst the deafening noise of another day will I return. The dewdrop is but a promise of the shower to come. And not unlike the dew am I. I too will return when my journey gathers me like a cloud pouring heavenly offerings on the earth.

I have returned to you for only a moment. But how long is a lifetime in the eye of eternity? I have spent time enough to search your souls and feel the rhythm of your hearts beating unto my own. What flesh conceals, spirit confesses. Often you despise your own eyes when unable to see the path beneath your feet. Soon you will not curse darkness in hopes of being blessed by light. The light lives only in the darkness.

Of this I am certain: within you burns a fire. And its blaze set my spirit free while I sat in prison. For my captivity was consumed as your words spoke to me. Your letters liberated my heart and mind from behind the iron bars where I was caged. And the fire in you forged the wings now fastened to my soul. If any Truth has taken flight this day, it is the outgrowth of that love you sent soaring in me. A short while, and my longing will gather dust to form the flesh of another body.

Like the leaves of a vast tree with infinite roots and branches, We are and so I am. To measure the tree by its overripe and fallen fruit is to reckon the power of a candle by the frailty of its wick. Rather than by how it sparks the flame that feeds a village or brings an empire to ruin. Until then, know the answer to every question you ask has always lived within you. Farewell to you and this blessed hour we have been given together.

Upon saying these things, the Poet heard the sirens sounding closer. And he spoke saying, *Those who once abducted me now approach ever more impatient. They will not wait much longer. And though they come with great numbers, their shackles will never again grasp and sever my flesh. I will not be captured and caged in another dungeon. Fare you well, People of Medina. What was given us here I will hold in my heart ever more. Forget not that I will return. Although the soul can be caged, it cannot be destroyed.*

And when the Poet had spoken his last word, he walked into the bonfire. But somehow he was not consumed. Rather he seemed to vanish into the flames. Or perhaps the flames vanished into him. For after he stepped into the inferno, the fire turned to smoke and suddenly burned no more. Then a cry came from the villagers who had crowded around as if from a single voice. And it shook the earth as the winds howled throughout the village.

Seven days and seven nights passed before the people of Medina would be moved from that sacred ground where a prophet was said to have risen into the heavens. And though the village streets and subways were all but empty on that seventh night, Priestess Hamida walked to and fro meditating within her heart on the words of her beloved: *Like the leaves of a vast tree with infinite roots and branches...*

We are and so I am.

AFTERWORD

Scripture says there is nothing new under the sun. Long before the gospel spoke of Madonna and Child, Isis mothered Horus in the ink-stained papyrus of ancient Kemet. By remixing old stories into the new, we keep alive the fires that have guided us along our way.

I was born just minutes from the block parties DJ's started in the South Bronx spinning old records over twin turntables. To a soundtrack of call-and-response shout outs over break beats, my brothers and I checked B-girls defying gravity as they resurrected Angolan dance rituals on subway trains from Times Square to Eastern Parkway. Graffiti writers paid homage to hieroglyphs from Queenbridge project walls to the Staten Island ferry. Street prophets moved crowds with verses Harlem heard in the revolutionary lyrics of The Last Poets. Folks treated inhumanely by the world's most powerful nation found ways to spit, break, tag and scratch centuries of struggle into the most popular cultural movement in human history. This book is written in tribute to the legacy of a poet from a time and place far from the birth of hip hop, but whose influence transcends geographic and generational boundaries no less.

For more than eight decades, Kahlil Gibran has enraptured millions around the world. With the exception of the Bible and the Koran, his 1923 masterpiece reportedly outsold all other 20th century books. Just as the rebel spirit of rap legends like Rakim and KRS-ONE were said to be pushing a passing fad in the 1980's, Gibran was once written off as a writer of no more than "meaningless mysticism." Despite the haters of his early writings, while living in New York City during a period leading to the Harlem Renaissance (1912-

1931) he catalyzed the birth of a new movement in the literature of his native land. Pushing for a global spiritual revolution, this man from Lebanon called for the world to reexamine not only the divide between East and West, but between the sacred and the secular. Refusing to be boxed into any single tradition, Gibran's work joins together the Judeo-Christian and Islamic traditions linked inextricably by his nation and family.

While studying in the same Boston winters Gibran immigrated to from his native Bisharri, I began those cold days listening to recordings of his masterpiece set to music. Challenging us all with passion, insight, grace and beauty, his verse made me more alive, at times envious, and always deeply inspired. I imagined how his story might be told if set under the towering skyscrapers in the concrete village of my birth. What if his prophet were not rescued from that mythical island where he was stranded, but instead returning home from Rikers Island prison? While teaching incarcerated youth on the world's largest penal colony, I wondered what a modern-day prophet in Brooklyn might say to us on the day of his release?

Life, observed Gibran, is conceived in the mist and not in the crystal. The spiritual awakening and political uprisings we are in the midst of today possess the power to re-write this world with the Word. Our poets are oral tradition ambassadors to generations past and yet to come. We set the language of worlds ancient and urban to music as one. Our poetry is both the verse of our time and a passport to the worlds we must forge. Some of us represent ourselves by re-presenting the stories of ancestors who lit the path before us. And so, this is the remix.

Bryonn Bain
March 20, 2011
Brooklyn, New York